Being an Astronaut

by Ginny Grissom

Editorial Offices: Glenview, Illinois • Parsippany, New Jersey • New York, New York
Sales Offices: Needham, Massachusetts • Duluth, Georgia • Glenview, Illinois
Coppell, Texas • Ontario, California • Mesa, Arizona

Astronauts work together on a spaceship.

Who can be an astronaut?

A man or a woman can be an astronaut. A pilot or a scientist can be an astronaut.

Astronauts eat on the spaceship *Endeavour.*

How do astronauts eat?

Food comes in special packs. Astronauts add water. Then they eat right out of the pack.

Spacesuits must move with the astronaut's body.

What do astronauts wear?

An astronaut could not live in space without a spacesuit. A spacesuit helps an astronaut stay warm in space. A spacesuit gives an astronaut air.

There is no up or down in space. You can even sleep standing on your head.

Where do astronauts sleep?

Some astronauts sleep in sleeping bags. Other astronauts sleep in beds. Some just find a quiet spot to rest.

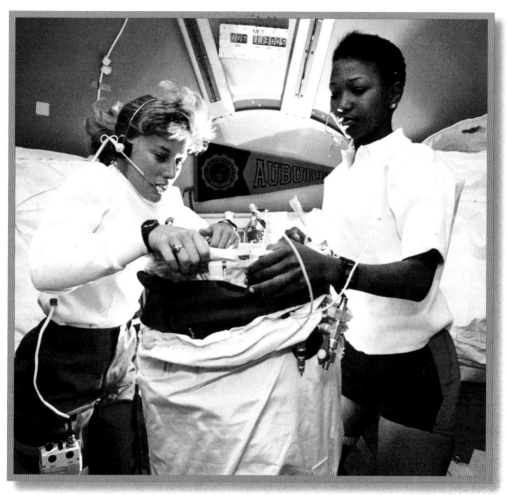

Astronauts do experiments in space.

What work do astronauts do?

Many astronauts build or fix machines. Some astronauts do science experiments.

An astronaut has a special view of our world.

Can an astronaut call home?

Astronauts can call everywhere. They can use computers to call home. They can say, "I love you."